CLIMBING
WITH
ABRAHAM

30 Devotionals to Help You Grow Your Faith, Build Your Life, and Discover God's Calling

David Ramos

Thank You!

I appreciate you taking the time to check out my book. As a thank you, I would like to send you the gift *Dreaming with Joseph: 12 Devotionals to Inspire Your Faith, Encourage Your Heart, and Help Your Realize God's Plan.*

To claim your free copy simply go to RamosAuthor.com and enter your email address.

Table of Contents

Introduction   1

A Bigger Story   3

A Better Perspective   5

Invincible Promises   7

Burdened by Grace   9

Bigger Than Us   11

Not Our Glory   13

Melchizedek's Example   15

Holy Frustration   17

Building Altars   19

No Shortcuts   21

The God Who Sees   23

Our Promise-Keeper   25

A Difficult Sign   27

The Ripple Effect   31

Is Anything Too Difficult?   35

Invitation for Compassion   39

Prayer Works   41

Memory Versus Fear   43

Promises Fulfilled   47

Our Messy God   49

Patience and Risk   53

Our Faithful Provider   57

The Most Powerful Force for Change   61

Love and Honor Part 1   65

Love and Honor Part 2   69

Legacy of Trust   73

Infectious Faith   77

Imagining Greatness   81

Lord, Lead Me   83

Stories of Faith   85

Continuing the Journey   87

About the Author

More Books by David Ramos

Further Reading on Abraham

Takeaway List

Acknowledgements

Endnotes

Introduction

I'm sure the first time I heard the story of Abraham was in Sunday school. But the first time I HEARD his story wasn't until my third year of college.

I was in a frustrating place – stuck by a lot of factors outside of my control. I found myself praying the same prayers over and over again for months at a time with nothing changing. I began to ask the questions every Christian asks during times like those: *what am I doing wrong, does God even hear me, why is this happening to me?*

It was during this time God turned my attention to Genesis. The stories in Genesis show a huge God, a Creator God, and caring God. It's within this magnificent book we find the character of Abraham.

Abraham was a man fighting his own frustrations as well. God grabs a hold of his life and completely redirects it, sending him into a strange land to fulfill impossible promises. During his journey Abraham faces war, barrenness, exploitation, and death. But he is also gifted with wealth, family and a famous legacy.

Abraham was far from perfect, but that never stopped the plans God had for him. The story of Abraham showed me how relentless our God is when it comes to accomplishing his amazing plans. God took an unknown foreigner and transformed him into the father of nations.

Abraham's climb to maturity and success was riddled with struggles and setbacks, much like our own. The key to his success, and the secret to ours, was an unwavering trust in the Almighty God.

I wrote this book first and foremost as a reminder to myself. I wanted to remember the God Abraham risked everything for, the God he praised when his wife Sarah finally gave birth, and the God he obeyed as he laid that child down as a sacrifice.

It's that kind of faith that sets one apart for greatness. The kind of faith that makes outsiders look in with awe and ask *how did they do that?* I want to live a life that doesn't make sense apart from God.

Today you have the opportunity to live a life like that. A life of furious, tremendous faith that invites God into every area and expects him to show up in huge ways! Reading through the life of Abraham can help us get there. Great faith is built one day at a time, step by step.

Your journey starts today. Now we begin the climb with Abraham.

A Bigger Story

Terah was the father of Abram, Nahor and Haran. Chapter 11 recounts hundreds of years of family lines down to when our main character, Abraham, was finally born. This illuminates a key point in Abraham's life and in the lives of all Christians.

Over and over again, the Bible begins a person's story by telling where they came from, who their parents were and what land they originally inhabited. This is all to show that our story begins long before we do.

Before Abraham ever lay Isaac on the altar, before he married Sarah or traveled to Egypt or even heard the voice of God, God was planning his story. God knew He would bless the nations through this one man. He knew Abraham would be a very important marker in the long, beautiful story of human salvation. But God also knew that, as important as Abraham's story was, he was still only a part of something much larger.

As you prepare to dive into the life of Abraham and discover the amazing truths hidden in his trials and triumphs, remember this one truth: there was a before Abraham and an after Abraham, and the same is true for you. Countless stories have taken place to allow you to live at this precise moment in time. Countless more will be written after you are gone.

Your story is part of something infinitely larger.

This is both freeing and frustrating. On one hand, we don't have to feel the pressure to be perfect. As we'll see, Abraham certainly was not. But at the same time, when trials arise, it feels like God could not care less about our little problems – we're just a small piece of the puzzle right? Not true.

<u>We are God's children, God's chosen.</u> To God, we are every ounce as important as Abraham, and he will take care of us with the same amount of care and love and power as He did for Abraham over 4,000 years ago.

Takeaway: My story is part of a much bigger story.

Prayer: Thank you, God, for choosing to include me in Your enormous plans. Bless me with humility and patience as I learn to discover and fulfill the call You have given me.

My life is important - it is a part of a bigger story!

A Better Perspective

Chapter 12 officially starts Abraham's epic story. He receives a blessing directly from God. He is promised a legacy, a family, and a meaningful purpose. As the verses continue, we see Abraham traveling, adhering to God's direction to "go," and confidently walking through expansive areas of the land he has been promised.

To outsiders, Abraham probably looked like another aimless wanderer. He had a fair amount of possessions and people with him, but he had no claim on the land he was traveling through. To God and Abraham, he was beginning the journey of promise, catching a glimpse of the promises God said He was going to fulfill.

Here, perspective is everything. If we are unclear about what God is doing in our lives (which is usually the case) we can fall prey to the outsider's view of the situation.

How did I get here? When is God going to do something? When we find ourselves stuck in situations like these, it's a good idea to go back and

5

read about the lives of the great men who have come before us, like Abraham – who walked through a land he did not own but was promised, and loved a woman who could not conceive, and trusted a God who would not hurry. You might feel lost or stuck, but you are not. God always fulfills his promises. He always does what is best for His children. And He always does so according to His own perfect timeline.

Take Abraham's view and choose to remember that God is at work, that you matter to God, and that you are not just wandering.

Takeaway: My perspective of every situation will either encourage or dishearten my trust in God.

Prayer: Help me to see that You are at work, Lord. Give me the right perspective, so that I can have peace and confidence in Your promises.

Invincible Promises

After Abraham received the promise, one of the first stories we read is of his failure to trust in God.

A famine fell upon the land that Abraham inhabited, and he was forced to travel down to Egypt. Out of fear of what the Pharaoh might do, Abraham concocted a half-lie saying that Sarah was his sister and not his wife *(even though she was technically his half-sister)*. He did this to protect his own life and even benefited from his lie. But everything quickly imploded. Pharaoh and his leaders were inflicted by a disease and cast Abraham and his wife out of the land along with all their belongings.

God communicates two incredibly powerful truths in this short story. First, all of God's chosen will make mistakes. I will, you will, Abraham certainly did. If the Bible repeats any message, it's that people will fail. You will at some point do something stupid or act out of fear, and the beautiful thing is – it's okay. It can be okay because of the second truth God communicates through this tale: His promises will not fail.

Despite Abraham's lack of faith, God didn't just write him off. God stepped in, intervened, and got Abraham back onto the path he was supposed to be on. What's crazy is that this isn't even the last time Abraham pulls this trick. Eight chapters later we'll see that this patriarch made the exact same mistake!

The purpose of this story, and I believe the whole of Abraham's life as well, is to give us hope. Hope and confidence that God's patience is more powerful than our stumbles, and His love is as strong as we are fragile. It's because of us that we often find our faces in the dirt. It's because of God that we can dust ourselves off, stand back up, and carry on even stronger than we were before.

Takeaway: God knows I will make mistakes, but His promises are invincible.

Prayer: Thank you Lord for being patient with me. Help me to avoid human failures. And when I fail, give me the confidence to come back to You, because I know You will not give up on me.

Burdened by Grace

Day 4
Genesis 13:1-13

A dark foreshadowing occurs in this section regarding Abraham's nephew, Lot. Up until this point, the two men and their tribes were traveling together, sharing resources as they went. But a quarrel broke out between the herdsmen of these two groups. To deal with this, Abraham chose a peaceful solution: allow Lot to choose a portion of the land and settle in it as his own.

What most readers miss in this passage is the loss Abraham must have felt sending Lot away. After Lot's father Haran died, it's likely that Abraham became his guardian or adopted father, which would have, in turn, made Lot his heir. Abraham saw his nephew as a very likely candidate to receive all the future promises from God: land, a nation, and countless descendants.

However, that was not the plan. Lot's people struck up a conflict with Abraham's group and likely brought upon themselves the darkest line of God's promise to Abraham: "those who curse you I will curse." Lot moved to greener lands near Sodom, and as we shall see, suffered for it.

The people we are responsible for often play a role in influencing our lives. Many times the consequences of their actions fall upon us. Whether it be our children, our employees, or even the people we associate with. Take care of how you lead those in your life, even if you were never given the title of "leader." As people of God, we are graced with immense power, and simultaneously burdened by immeasurable responsibility.

Takeaway: As a child of God I am responsible for more than just myself.

Prayer: Father, help me to respect the spiritual authority You have given me as one of Your chosen. Help me to lead with wisdom, patience, and forgiveness.

Bigger Than Us

Day 5
Genesis 13:14-18

Here, the Lord reiterates His promises to Abraham, only this time with a greater magnitude. Abraham is promised all the land he can see, from the mountains to the waters and every valley in between. Furthermore, he is promised an innumerable number of descendants to inhabit it. God then urges him to walk through the land. Abraham follows His directions and responds by building an altar to worship God.

It's inspiring to see Abraham get such a powerful and direct promise from God. But for anyone who knows how the rest of the story goes, it's also incredibly frustrating. Abraham had to wait decades until his son Isaac was born. And of all the land he was promised, he only ends up legally owning a fraction of one percent of it by his death – for which he was probably overcharged.

Anyone reading this story with an honest heart has to ask the question, *Why is God so slow, or bad, at keeping His promises?* It's not a subject we like to address, but it's one every one of us as Christians will face in our lives...when will God step in and do something?

If the story of Abraham reminds us of any truth, it's that God's plans are always incomprehensibly larger than our own. God didn't make promises to Abraham because He just wanted to help the guy out. God brought Abraham into an extraordinary epic, the salvation of mankind.

God's promises to the single man of Abraham were meant to bring about much more than Abraham could ever imagine – descendants that grew into the nation of Israel, the Israelite who birthed the Son of God, and the Christ who died, and will return for his bride, the Church.

God cares for you intimately, but is never thinking of only you. His plans are always bigger than us, and that is for our ultimate good.

Takeaway: It's okay to get frustrated when God doesn't seem to be keeping His promises. He's working on something big and has not forgotten about you.

Prayer: God, thank You for keeping Your promises. Please give me the patience and faith to know that You are at work, and that I can trust Your ultimate plan for me.

Not Our Glory

Day 6
Genesis 14:11-17; 21-24

The peace of Abraham's story has been disrupted by the invasion of foreign kings. Their paths wouldn't likely have crossed, except that one of the prisoners the kings took during their campaign was Lot. So Abraham immediately rallied his small force (318 men would have certainly been a fraction of the force they were about to fight). With God on his side, Abraham was victorious and two of the defending kings came to give their thanks: Melchizedek and the unnamed king of Sodom.

Melchizedek's reaction was unique, as we will see tomorrow. But the king of Sodom reacted in an even stranger way. He was short, almost annoyed at the fact that he had to thank Abraham for saving his people. Abraham must have sensed that this man was ill-fated and so refused to have any of his own wealth tainted by Sodom's spoils.

Let's take a second to really see what Abraham was turning down. The force Abraham faced was likely multiple times larger than his own - in the thousands versus his own hundreds. We also know of at least two entire cities they had recently sacked.

13

Therefore, each one of the 318 men would have likely been set for life, each wealthy in his own right.

However, Abraham chooses a different path. With at least 318 fighting men behind him, Abraham was certainly not lacking. By this time he was likely moderately wealthy as well. We can guess as to the exact reason why Abraham refused to take the spoils of war, which were rightfully his, but I suspect it had to do with Godly pride.

God was the reason he had come so far and still had so many promises to look forward to. Abraham wanted to keep that truth pure. He wanted outsiders to see that God was the sole reason for his success.

Few of us will ever be faced with the temptation of great wealth, but what we will have to face is the integrity of our testimony. If outsiders were to look at our lives, would it be clear that we chose the decisions that honored God, even when they were the more difficult or less rewarding options? Do our choices show greater allegiance to God's glory, or our own?

Takeaway: Sometimes choosing God's best requires us to give up our immediate good.

Prayer: Remind me, Lord, that You are my source, my provider, and my champion. I was made for Your glory, not my own.

Melchizedek's Example

Day 7
Genesis 14:18-20

A lot has been made of these few verses. Who is Melchizedek really? Why is he so important in later scriptures? Why would Abraham give him a tenth? And how did he come to worship the One True God?

For our purpose, we want to pay attention to what Melchizedek had to do with Abraham's story. In short, not much. It's likely he approached Abraham alongside the king of Sodom, who you read about yesterday. Both had a very different response to Abraham, and consequently, God had a very different response to them.

No one can say for sure who Melchizedek was exactly, or how he came to serve the same God as Abraham. What is clear is that when Melchizedek declared a blessing over Abraham and served him a royal dinner (bread and wine), he invoked the blessing of God upon himself.

Here we see one of the promises made to Abraham come true: "I will bless those who bless you." Melchizedek went on to become a very important symbol for Christ in the Old Testament. I can't help but believe that was a result of his treatment of Abraham. Because he took a risk in front of his fellow kings and blessed this foreigner, God rewarded him. First, through a tenth of Abraham's spoils. Second, through a legacy of being remembered as a great servant of God.

Who has God called you to bless, to stand up for, to defend, to clothe, to encourage? I believe deeply that God is most satisfied when He sees His children helping one another. And when God is satisfied, He cannot help but bless.

Takeaway: God blesses us when we help fellow believers.

Prayer: I know You look out for Your children, and sometimes You do that through ordinary people like me. Please give me eyes to see opportunities to help others and the courage to follow through.

Holy Frustration

Day 8
Genesis 15:1-6

Abraham is frustrated. He doesn't want to hear platitudes or empty reassurances. By this point in the story he is old, past the normal age of fatherhood and likely past the physical possibility of it as well.

He wants something God promised him: a child. God hears his frustration and reminds him that He keeps His promises. Abraham will have a child, of his own flesh, who will be his heir and carry out the promises of God. Whereas we might still want to argue with God and beg Him for a more specific answer, Abraham doesn't. He falls silent, not out of defeat but out of belief. He trusts that God will fulfill His word, a righteous act.

I have never met an honest Christian who has not been, at least once, severely frustrated with God. More than a handful of times I have found myself yelling at Him, fuming at the injustices He has allowed into my life.

This snippet of Abraham's journey reminds me that this is normal. As people of God, we should be pushing the limits of our lives and making big hopes.

If there is no possibility of failure then there is no evidence of faith. At every stage in life we will be wanting for something: healing, employment, peace, direction, hope. And at every stage we will be faced with the question, *Am I going to believe God in this?*

God knew what He was doing. He planned when Isaac would come into the world, down to the millisecond. He takes the same care with how He answers our prayers. Down to the millisecond, God knows when He will step in with a yes; or, with all the tenderness of a loving parent, He knows how to endure our tantrums when His answer is no.

Takeaway: God knows your frustration; keep believing.

Prayer: I want to know that You are listening, Lord... that You care. Restore my hope in You.

Building Altars

Abraham begins this section with another question for God: *How can I know*? This time he is referring to the promise of inheriting the Promised Land. God answers by having Abraham prepare a sacrifice. Once he does so, the Lord appears with the imagery of fire and smoke and solidifies His promise to Abraham as a covenant.

This section also ties strong parallels to Israel's future as an enslaved nation. God assures their eventual freedom to Abraham and goes on to list in detail the lands they will inhabit.

One thing highlighted in these verses is the physical reminders of God's promises. Abraham prepares a physical sacrifice and literally sees the spirit of God interact with it. The Israelites exit Egypt with great possessions, marking not only the beginning of their new lives but also the faithfulness of God throughout their enslavement.

Somewhere along the way, many of us have been convinced that physical reminders of God's promises show a lack of faith. On the contrary, time and time again the Bible shows us men and women building altars as remembrance for something God did in their lives.

I have two "altars." First, a twenty-dollar bill tucked near the bottom of my dresser drawer as a reminder that God always provides. Second, a war-torn Bible with the cover missing that has this quote scribbled on its front page: "A Bible that's falling apart usually belongs to someone who isn't" – Charles H. Spurgeon.

Take time today to find or make something that will act as a physical reminder of God's faithfulness.

Takeaway: It's okay to ask God, *How can I know?* Faith doesn't always have to be invisible.

Prayer: Thank you Lord for Your promises. Please encourage my faith today with something tangible.

No Shortcuts

Day 10
Genesis 16:1-6

Sarah was a woman of God. She had seen, time and time again, how God had miraculously provided, saved, and promoted her husband Abraham. But the lack of one thing continued to eat at her: a child. At this point in the story, the promise of an heir had probably weighed heavily on Sarah's shoulders for many years. She wanted to perform for her husband. Child-bearing was a top priority for women in that age and if they could not have children, they were often seen as cursed.

Sarah refused to wait any longer and decided to take matters into her own hands. Her idea was a perfectly legal solution to the problem. She would give Hagar, her servant, to Abraham, and the child Hagar bore would belong to Sarah. The maid would be nothing more than a tool in the whole plot.

Abraham was likely just as confused and frustrated as his wife was at the situation so he agreed to her plan. Like Adam taking the fruit from Eve, so Abraham lay with Hagar at his wife's behest. As you could have guessed, Sarah's impatience and rash decision led to an explosive end. The two women became violent towards one another once Hagar was with child. The maid couldn't take it anymore and decided to run away. When this happened, everyone felt the loss, "Hagar has lost her home, Sarai her maid, and Abram his second wife and newborn child."[i]

Here, the Bible reminds us that even those closest to us will sometimes tempt us to circumvent God's plan with a logical answer. Having a surrogate mother was the logical answer to Sarah's infertility. But God had other plans. He assured Abraham that the child would come from his own body, inferring that Sarah was equally as important in the plan. Their impatience trumped God's promise and disaster was the result.

Takeaway: God's plans are not always logical, but they are the best option.

Prayer: Help me to trust You God and to be patient with Your plan, even when the way You choose to do things doesn't make sense to me.

The God Who Sees

This is a painful scene to read. Abraham washed his hands of the conflict between Sarah and Hagar, and it escalated to the point of Hagar fearing for her life. She did what any person, and soon-to-be mother, would do – she ran away to protect her child and herself. This is where something incredible happens.

Hagar is alone in the desert, forgotten and abandoned. She was a pregnant foreigner, easy pickings for any bad folk in the area. But God planned otherwise. He entered simply and beautifully. He saw her when no one else did, and cared for her when no one else would.

The stories of great women and men in the Bible are meant to peel away the covering of who God really is. Of all the names God is given in Genesis, this one is my favorite: El Roi – the God who sees me.

When we pray it often feels like we're talking to nothing, like our prayers are bouncing off the walls, and our struggles are invisible to the One who could help. They're not. We're not invisible. You are not stuck, you are not forgotten, and you are not hopeless.

We serve a God who sees. We serve a God who hears. We serve a God who is jealously vying for our attention, beckoning us to stop settling because He has so much more in store for His children. Don't you think that sort of God, that kind of Father, would listen to you when you cry out in pain? Don't you think the God who takes the time to watch an animal (Job 39:1) would turn His eyes towards you when you ask?

God is the ultimate Good Samaritan: what He sees He must take action on, and He sees you.

Takeaway: God sees me, and what He sees He takes action on.

Prayer: Thank You Lord that, no matter what I am going through, I can have hope because I know You see what is happening. Help me, Amen.

Our Promise-Keeper

Day 12
Genesis 17:1-8

Something happens here that changes the entire scale of the story. Up until this point we knew that Abraham was promised land and a descendant who would eventually become a nation. But God takes all of His promises to the next level. Instead of one nation, many will come from him; and instead of just all the land he could see, his descendants will possess the whole land forever! To confirm these increased promises, God changes his faithful servant's name from Abram to Abraham, which in Hebrew signifies the grander scale of his fate.

So much is happening here and it is all prefaced by the first sentence of the chapter: "When Abram was ninety-nine." As if the promises weren't impossible enough, they are being given to a very old man.

Abraham's story depends entirely on God showing up. Abraham is old. He has no power to heal his wife's barrenness, let alone live long enough to lead his children into battle to claim the land. All Abraham can do at this point is thank God, and continue living his normal, faithful life. He has no power to bring the promises of God to pass.

Neither do we. Our lives are always in God's hands. What He wants to do with us depends on His grace, His timing, and His purpose. This often frustrates me because I want to make things happen. I want to hurry things along and live a bigger, better, more influential life for God. But, like Abraham, our story depends entirely on God showing up.

Maybe the promise God has over your life is not as grand as fathering nations, but it is important. One of the greatest tools we have as Christians to change the world is the promises of God, but the only way to use those promises is to patiently trust God that He will use us to accomplish them.

Takeaway: Only God can fulfill the promises He makes.

Prayer: Help me to know the promises You have placed on my life Lord, and give me patience as You see them through.

A Difficult Sign

Day 13
Genesis 17:9-14

We just read about all the incredible things God promised to do for Abraham: how he will be great and numerous and how God will make these blessings come to fruition. Then we enter the second half of the covenantal agreement. Abraham must do something to hold up his side of the bargain: circumcision. This condition is not optional.

As you could imagine, Abraham and the grown men who are a part of his group are not jumping for joy at the idea of taking a knife to their most precious body part. So why does God do this?

Circumcision is meant to be a sign. Just like the rainbow was a sign to Noah or the Passover meal a sign to the rescued Israelites. This act is a physical reminder to Abraham and his descendants that God promised He would do something and if they want to be a part of it, they must do this one thing.

You too must do one thing if you are to become a part of what God has promised, and that is believe in His Son Jesus Christ.

Abraham didn't have a "savior" yet. He was serving a God very few knew about let alone cared for. Think how ridiculous some of his men and descendants probably thought this ritual was – *You want me to do what?!* However, all of this was paving the way toward events Abraham could have never conceived happening, let alone discovering he was a major pillar in their coming true.

As you grow in your faith and live out this frustrating, beautiful, confusing, adventurous thing called the Christian life, you will inevitably be faced with circumcision events. God will ask you to do things that do not make sense and that will probably hurt in the short term.

Our job, like Abraham, is not to figure out exactly how all of this is going to work and why it had to be done this way. Our role is much simpler, albeit more difficult: to trust God.

I can't help but think that all of those in Abraham's care respected him to such a degree, that when they saw their leader undergo circumcision at his ripe old age, nearly all of them followed without argument. They trusted his faith and he trusted God. That is the sort of person I want to become.

Takeaway: God will ask difficult things of us at times; trust Him anyways.

Prayer: Thank you that Jesus is the reason I can believe in the promises of God. When You ask hard things of me, please give me the faith to follow through.

The Ripple Effect

Day 14
Genesis 17:15-27

God does not stop talking after He describes the conditions of the covenant to Abraham. Instead, He keeps speaking, and what He says is incredible.

He continues by explaining how His blessing will overflow and impact everyone else in Abraham's life: Sarah will give birth and become the mother of nations, Isaac will carry the everlasting covenant, and Ishmael will father a host of rulers. The sweeping promises conclude with God rising back up to Heaven and Abraham immediately following through with circumcising all the men in his care, including himself.

A number of events stand out in importance in this section. First, Sarai's name is changed to Sarah. It's a much less drastic change than Abram to Abraham, but still it shows that she is as much a part of God's plan as her husband is.

Second, Abraham showed an instant of doubt. It's hard to blame him since he's been waiting over 20 years now for a son. But God does not reprimand him. Instead, He reaffirms His promise: Ishmael will

31

be blessed, but Isaac is the one they've all been waiting for. Finally, Abraham follows through, circumcising what would likely have been hundreds of men that very same day.

The promises God places on our lives will affect everyone around us. For Abraham, they impacted his wife, his children, his servants, and even his enemies. It's this reality that makes trusting God so much more difficult at times, because the consequences of our faith do not just fall on us, but also onto our mates, our children, or our employees.

As leaders, we bear the weight of responsibility for those placed under our care and we should never take that lightly. However, we also should never let that duty restrain us from taking risks for God and acting immediately on the things God has called us to do.

Everyone who was a part of Abraham's story faced the risk of things turning out badly. Traveling was dangerous, giving birth (especially at an old age) was dangerous, having all the men in your camp bedridden because of circumcision was dangerous. But at the same time, they were all blessed because of it. Sarah mothered a nation, Abraham entered a covenant, and all those men and women in their care became part of something eternally bigger than they could have imagined.

Takeaway: Our relationship with God affects everyone around us.

Prayer: Father, help me trust that You have not only my best in mind, but also the best for my family, for my friends, and for everyone You put under my care. Help me lead well.

Is Anything Too Difficult?

Day 15
Genesis 18:1-15

In today's passage, Abraham is met by three travelers. Hospitality towards guests was a very important part of the culture in that time, so Abraham spared no expense. The food he provided showed that he was a very generous and wealthy man (there would have been enough bread and meat to feed at least twice as many people).[ii] The heart of this story is how Abraham's actions contrast with the next chapter – how are these same guests treated as they enter the gates of Sodom and Gomorrah? You will see the parallels of that shortly.

For now, look at how Abraham was rewarded for the hospitality he provided. After the guests had eaten, they confirm the promise Abraham had just received a little while ago: he will have a son by Sarah. What's surprising is that Sarah laughs, just as Abraham did the first time he heard. That means, for whatever reason, Abraham had not yet shared the news with her. But God, in disguise as one of the visitors, answers Sarah's doubt: *Is anything too difficult for the Lord?*

That last phrase is the key of both Sarah's and Abraham's stories. Time and time again, they are faced with difficult circumstances and seemingly impossible situations. Yet every single time, God makes Himself present and asks the same question, whether explicitly or implicitly: *Is anything too difficult for me?*

God asks the same question of us during every trial we face. Financial problems, work issues, family drama, health scares – is anything too difficult for Him? The One who formed us in the womb can repair any broken body. The God who designed your exact gifts and personality knows why He made you that way, and He will give you work that gives you joy.

Over and over again, we're faced with situations bigger than us, and the temptation is to complain to God. Why are You letting this happen? Why aren't You doing anything?

He is doing something.

He is watching out for you. And it is not hard or stressful for Him. He knows exactly what He is doing. Your struggle is no surprise to Him and Your doubt does not slow Him down.

Once Sarah had Isaac she had a daily reminder that God can do the impossible. Let God's provision do the same for you.

Takeaway: Nothing is too difficult for God.

Prayer: Lord, help me to remember that You have my best in mind and that no matter what I am facing, You are infinitely bigger than my struggles.

Invitation for Compassion

Day 16
Genesis 18:16-33

By now, Abraham knows his three guests are divine and sees them off towards their next stop, the city of Sodom. Abraham overhears their discussion and begins to intercede on behalf of the city. These requests that Abraham makes are not light-hearted. Six times he pleads with the traveler who represents the Lord, *please do not destroy this city*. Each time the Lord lowers his requirement of righteous inhabitants: from 50 to 45, 40, 30, 20 and finally 10. The scene is left with an ominous tone – will they find 10 righteous people or will the city be destroyed?

Why would Abraham waste his time trying to save an evil city? If it was just out of concern for his nephew Lot, he could have just asked for the Lord to spare him. But he never even mentions his nephew.

Abraham is showing compassion in its truest form: undeserved and unselfish. God is acting to protect his people by getting rid of the disease in the region. He leaves the opportunity open to Abraham by letting him listen in. God wants Abraham to show compassion and ask for mercy for the city. The Lord is the One, then, who invites the opportunity for forgiveness for Sodom; Abraham just had to ask for it.

Do you see how incredibly powerful that makes our prayers? The Lord invited Abraham to change his mind, to alter His course and save an entire city. Abraham was just a man like you and me. We have been given the same power and influence over the events of this world, if we would only ask.

God is waiting for us to ask and pray for big things; opportunities to truly change our situation, our family, and our world.

Takeaway: God is inviting us to change this world.

Prayer: Thank You God that You have given us so much power in prayer. Give me the courage to make big asks, and eyes to see big change.

Prayer Works

Day 17
Genesis 19:27-29

Chapter 19 represents the worst case scenario come to fruition. The three men who met with Abraham just a few days before whittled down to two and entered Sodom. Lot tried his best to care for them as his uncle did, but the sins of the city overwhelmed the visitors. In a terrifying scene a mob forms and attacks Lot's home. Suddenly, the two strangers reveal their divine nature, blind the crowd, and scurry Lot's family to safety. Lot and his surviving daughters watch as fire rains down onto the place they once called home.

Abraham wakes up the next morning and looks to find a valley flooded with smoke. The people he pleaded for have all been destroyed. And what about his nephew Lot? It's not until much later he discovers Lot made it out alive.

What could Abraham have been feeling as he saw the pillars of smoke the next day? Anger, failure, frustration, helplessness...

Six times Abraham begged God to do something else, to not destroy them, and for what? Did God even listen? Yes.

Verse 29 says that God "remembered" Abraham and, for that reason, made the effort to save Lot and his family. Lot was not offered salvation because of his own merits but because of the merit of his uncle Abraham.

Who we are matters. Our character matters. And one day we might discover that it mattered a whole lot more than we could have ever imagined. God remembered Abraham's prayer because of who Abraham was. His prayer changed things, not in the way Abraham had hoped, but in such a way that three lives were spared that day.

Abraham saved someone's life because he was a good man and prayed. How much more power do we have since our merit is based on Christ?

Takeaway: Prayer works, just not always in the way we think it should.

Prayer: Lord, help me to become a person of character and of prayer and to know that Christ is my merit.

Memory Versus Fear

Day 18
Genesis 20:1-18

This story strikes a curious déjà vu for anyone familiar with the Abraham saga. Back in chapter 12, a similar situation takes place. Here Abraham finds himself in a new land once again. Yet, despite all the triumphs he has been a part of because of God's help, he still fears the king, Abimelech. To protect himself and his loved ones, Abraham repeats the lie from chapter 12, that Sarah and he are siblings and nothing more.

The king takes Sarah to be with him in his household, and a sickness falls upon everyone there. The disease is bad enough to make all the women in the household barren and Abimelech come to the brink of death. It is here that God intervenes. In a dream, He puts the king on trial and shows that it was His omnipotence that kept Abimelech from stumbling into greater sin. The king then calls Abraham to come answer for his lie.

The Abraham we see here is very different from the conquering patriarch of recent chapters. He's fearful and even timid in his responses. He let fear guide him. Abimelech answers by sending him away with a hefty amount of apologetic gifts. The chapter concludes with the Lord healing all the barren women, foreshadowing what is to come.

Have you ever had to take a test over? A redo? Maybe you failed the first time and were given a second chance to pass. Usually, when we are given an opportunity like this, we do much better the second time around. We remember what we got right the first time, and work to improve the items we got wrong.

So why isn't it this easy in real life? Have you ever found yourself in the same bind again, fighting the same bad habits, and making the choices you swore to yourself you'd never make again? Abraham's been there. By this point in his life he has seen God over and over again accomplish extraordinary feats: divine protection, destroying cities, and supernatural appearances. But none of this is enough to overrule the very real fear Abraham feels in that moment when he enters the new city.

We make this same mistake. We fail to learn from the lessons of the past because we let fear rule our thinking. Memory is the best antidote with which to fight fear. If Abraham would have remembered how God handled the situation in Egypt and how he was protected, he would have made better choices.

The same is true for us. The next time you find yourself in a situation where fear is guiding your choices, pause. Take a minute to remember a time when God intervened in a big way and use that memory to fuel your faith in this moment.

Takeaway: Remembering God's actions in our past will help us fight today's fear.

Prayer: Father, thank You for being so patient with me. Grow my faith by helping me to remember everything You have already done.

Promises Fulfilled

Day 19
Genesis 21:1-7

The impossible has happened. Sarah, barren and advanced in age, has just given birth to her first son, Isaac. It's exactly what she and Abraham had hoped for but had nearly given up on.

These verses recount that God had promised them this exact gift at this precise time. God kept His end of the bargain and, in response, Abraham followed by naming the child Isaac and circumcising him on the eighth day, just as God had commanded. Finally, Sarah releases words of joy: *Who would have thought this could have really happened to me?*

She is overwhelmed with happiness because in her eyes she has fulfilled a huge part of God's ultimate plan; the promises made to Abraham now have an heir to be fulfilled through.

God always fulfills His promises. He doesn't mind if they go against nature or circumstance. In fact, sometimes He prefers it that way.

You are no different than Sarah and Abraham. You are a person, a piece of creation God sees and loves and cares for. He knows what bothers you. He sympathizes with what wakes you up at night or stresses you out or eats at your peace. He made you for a purpose, and He has made promises to you to help you fulfill that purpose.

Abraham and Sarah waited a long time to see God fulfill His promise to them. Decades passed and still no son. They even tried to hurry the promise by having a son through Hagar, but that only caused more issues. Still, Abraham believed.

He kept his faith because he put it not in the promise itself but in the One making the promise. For years everything around him, even his own wife, was telling him this thing wasn't going to happen. It's just too hard, too big, too impossible. However, Abraham kept his eyes on the Promisor. He saw a God who was bigger than the problem, bigger than his doubts, and bigger than the circumstances.

Learn the promises God has made to you because He is incessantly working for your good (Matthew 6:25-26 is a good place to start.)

Takeaway: Put Your faith in the Promisor, and keep Your eyes on Him.

Prayer: Thank You God for always fulfilling Your promises. Please give me patience and peace to know that You are working.

Our Messy God

Day 20
Genesis 21:8-21

The scene in this chapter shifts dramatically from celebrating the birth and weaning of Isaac to watching Hagar and Ishmael come to the brink of death in the desert. Hagar and her son have always been a burden to Sarah, but now she's had enough and urges Abraham to send the slave away. Abraham is deeply bothered at the thought of never seeing his son again. God intervenes, but not in the way we expect. He advises Abraham to obey his wife and send them off, that He will be the one caring for them now.

Hagar and her son make it only a short time into the desert before the situation turns dangerous. Waterless and exhausted, the mother resigns herself to watching her son die before she dies too. Thankfully, God intervenes once more. He finds her in the desert as He did before and provides for them. They are saved and Ishmael goes on to become the man God had promised.

This short story is about as messy as it can get. To Sarah, Hagar likely represents failure and distrust. She did not need a reason to send her away but found one in her misbehaving son. Abraham is torn at the predicament because he does not see Ishmael as any less of a son to him than Isaac.

What's amazing is that God intervenes, not just once but twice. He tells Abraham what he should do and also works to save the mother and son duo in the desert for a second time. Of all the lessons hidden in this text, the one I keep coming back to is the reality that God does not run away from messes - He enters them.

Illegitimate children, family drama, inner turmoil, physical pain... all of these are human problems. They were brought about by the bad choices of people. Sarah should never have told Abraham to sleep with Hagar. Ishmael should never have picked on Isaac. Abraham shouldn't have let the turmoil in his family reach this point. It was their shared faults. But God acted anyway.

So often we can feel trapped by our own bad choices and rash decisions. Then, when we try to pray or ask for help, all we feel is a mountain of guilt. We're the ones who got ourselves into this mess, so we should be the ones to get ourselves out. God doesn't see it that way.

He sees our mess as His mess too and He is waiting for us to ask for help. He does not shy away from dishonorable situations. He rolls up His sleeves and dives in with both hands.

That's the God we serve and that's the God waiting for you to ask for help.

Takeaway: God doesn't run away from messes. He runs toward them.

Prayer: Thank you Lord for Your willingness to step into my messy life and make things better. I need Your help today.

Patience and Risk

Genesis 21:22-34

A child was not the only promise God made to his servant Abraham. Another key promise was the land. However, up until this point in the story, Abraham has been consistently a foreigner in other people's property. Here, that all changes.

Abimelech makes his second appearance into Abraham's story, this time to create a treaty with the growing patriarch. He sees God's favor upon the man and wants to both protect himself and benefit from it. Abraham also wants peace between their groups, but an issue has arisen. One of Abraham's wells had been taken by Abimelech's men. A well in those days represented much more than water - it was their lifeline in desert territory - what allowed them to grow their flocks and people. Taking one from a people group would have been a serious offense.

Abraham seizes the moment and uses the treaty as an opportunity to gain something even more valuable: a well of his own. Abimelech accepts his offer and the place of Beersheba is founded.

Abraham then plants a tree, further cementing his ownership of that piece of land.

For the first time, we see Abraham becoming a landowner. He was already rich, but now his new son Isaac has something more than money and servants to inherit; he has a place they can begin to call home.

Sometimes it feels like we wait for forever for God to fulfill His promises and for good things to happen. Abraham had been childless and landless for decades and then, all within one chapter, those pieces began to be fulfilled.

God does not forget His promises, and neither should we. Abraham didn't let the blessing of his new son take his eyes off everything God still had planned for him.

What are you hoping and waiting for? Don't be afraid to make big asks of God and then take big steps for them to come true. Abraham was faithful in two ways. First, by the consistency of his actions and second, by his willingness to take risks.

Beersheba was simply the prologue to all God was going to do with Abraham's descendants. It would never would have happened if he didn't believe in and act towards the promises of God.

Takeaway: God's promises require both patience and action.

Prayer: God, help me to know when You want me to rise up and fight for what You are giving me, and when to hold back and wait on Your perfect timing.

Our Faithful Provider

Day 22
Genesis 22:1-8

Everything slows to a snail's pace as chapter 22 begins. The last few chapters have catalogued decades of the patriarch's life, but now the entire chapter covers only a few days to emphasize their relative importance.

God decides to test Abraham by asking him to sacrifice his son, Isaac. He uses extra words to convey the importance of Isaac to Abraham (*your only son, whom you love*). While human sacrifice would have been looked down upon, it wasn't unheard of in that time. Abraham saddled his donkey with the very real expectation that he may not be coming back with his son alive.

They continued on until they came upon the mountain God had ordained. As Abraham and his son begin to climb, a curious Isaac asks what they will be sacrificing. A hopeful, heavy-hearted Abraham replies that God will provide.

Think of all the questions that must have been swirling around Abraham's head during all of this: why would God ask this of me? How is He going to keep His promises if Isaac is dead? What did I do to deserve this? Would God really go through with this?

I imagine that climb had to be the hardest moment of Abraham's life. Everything he had hoped and prayed and waited for was now about to be laid down on an altar. He would have to give the boy back to God in the worst way: by killing him himself.

Yet through all this, Abraham is consistently obedient and hopeful. He doesn't wait a week or a month to think about it. Instead, he leaves the very next morning. He doesn't give himself time to let doubt or fear change his mind. He moves, trusting that the same God who brought him this far will continue to take care of him in every way. And so he continued to climb to the designated place.

You will be asked to climb too, at some time during your walk with Christ. It is for great reasons God asks impossible things of His servants. But when we are asked, we won't be able to see the greatness through the pain. All Abraham could see was the possibility that his son might die. However, he was able to keep his hope by remembering that God had always provided: wealth, land, riches and so much more.

When God asks great things of you, you will only see His request as a loss on your part unless you remember that He is your provider and that whatever He is doing will benefit you more than it hurts you in the end.

As we will see tomorrow, Abraham's worst fear did not come true because, just as he hoped would happen, God provided.

Takeaway: God is our ultimate provider. God's actions are always for our provision.

Prayer: Lord, when You ask difficult things of me please remind me that this too will somehow work out for my good.

The Most Powerful Force for Change

Day 23
Genesis 22:9-19

The climb is over. Abraham and Isaac are high up on the mountain and begin to prepare the altar. During this preparation, Isaac does not run; he does not complain or question. Just as Abraham completely trusts God, so Isaac trusts his father, and he lets Abraham bind him with rope.

With urgency, God interrupts and tells Abraham to drop everything. These actions have proven that Abraham holds nothing higher than God, not even his only son. To affirm his pleasure and role as provider, God brings a ram to be sacrificed in Isaac's stead. The powerful section closes with God swearing to fulfill His promises to an even greater extent: Abraham's descendants will be incredibly numerous and victorious thanks to this day, when the will of God intersected with the obedience of man.

The whole scene is emotionally overwhelming. Abraham is at first feeling intense fear and anxiety that his son may die, then a second wave of relief and joy washes over him as God provides an alternate sacrifice. But before he can digest anything that has just occurred he is deeply humbled and likely in awe that God would swear by Himself a promise to him. Finally, another wave of relief and joy comes as he descends the mountain, thankful that he has just triumphed over the most difficult task of his life.

This is most often what it looks and feels like to obey God. It may begin in a place of hope or confidence but quickly falls into fear and anxiety as trouble arises. For whatever reason, we still like to believe that the path God has for us is the one with the least amount of potholes and thieves. Not true.

Whenever God asks us to walk a certain way, it is usually for two reasons: first, because the destination will be much better, and second, because the journey will grow us; both things that will be preceded by difficulty.

As we continue in obedience there will be moments of relief and humility. There will be times when God reaffirms that He is working for us and not against us. We will have seasons of rest, where God answers our prayers, provides in some miraculous way, or just gives us a deep peace to know that we are headed in the right direction.

Obedience to God is not straightforward. It doesn't always feel good or make the most sense. However, when the perfect will of God meets the complete obedience of man, it is the most powerful force for change on earth.

Takeaway: My obedience, while difficult, is an incredibly powerful tool for God.

Prayer: Give me the endurance to be obedient to Your will, God, especially when it doesn't make sense to me.

Love and Honor Part 1

Day 24
Genesis 23:1-2

After years of struggle, joy, unrest and finally motherhood, Sarah passes away. She is one of the most respected women of the Old Testament, and it's easy to see why. She continued to rely on God even in the most difficult circumstances: barrenness, being put in another man's house twice, following her husband even when the direction he chose was odd or flat out wrong. But she continued diligently and prayerfully. She was by no means perfect; her battles with Hagar and laughter in the face of God prove that point. But she was a woman fully devoted to God, faults and all. And for that we honor her as Abraham did.

Abraham lost his lifelong best friend. For years they were tied together by the promises of God – together holding one another accountable and helping each other through the periods of doubt. Without Sarah, Abraham would have never become the man we know as the patriarch of Israel. He knew that, which is why he mourned her so deeply.

It's his love that sets up the scene for the rest of this chapter. His desire to honor her and keep his

65

promises to Sarah is what prompts him to enter the conversation he has in the proceeding verses. He wages to secure land on her behalf in order to give her a proper burial, and in doing so, plants the seeds of ownership which will fulfill future promises.

I, myself, am engaged, and I can honestly say that I am a better man for pursuing the woman I believe God placed in my life. This is not a statement about soul mates or true love. Instead, what I believe Abraham's relationship with Sarah shows us is the potential fruit of faithful service to one another.

Together they made incredible mistakes – lying, cheating, disbelief, anger, and so much more. Yet, together they also had Isaac, and followed God for decades, and built the foundations of what would become the great people of Israel. Abraham served Sarah, and she him, and out of that service birthed a love and respect that enabled them to become the best versions of themselves.

If you are married, take today to thank God for everything your spouse does and is for you. Spouses are a gift in the truest sense of the word, and when we make Christ the priority in our relationship with them, amazing things can happen.

For those who are not yet married, take today to honor a couple in your life that exemplifies a godly marriage. Take note of what they do and don't do, of what they say and how they treat each other. Because one day you may be called to protect and honor someone in the same way, just as Abraham and Sarah did for one another all those years ago.

Takeaway: Marriage can be a tool for helping us fulfill the promises of God.

Prayer: Thank you for this beautiful thing called marriage – and how it shows Your love towards us more than anything. Help me do it well.

Love and Honor Part 2

Day 25
Genesis 23:3-20

Prompted by the need for a proper burial site for his beloved wife, Abraham moves into negotiations with the elder Hittites to secure a piece of land. Clearly, they know who he is. Abraham has made a name for himself over the last few decades because of his victories and wealth. Because of that, they try to honor him by simply giving him the land he has requested. The nuance here is that land given would still technically belong to the giver, more like a loan than a true gift.[iii] However, Abraham has not come here to merely borrow something. He has come to solidify his right to be there by owning a piece of land himself and burying his wife in a place that would finally be called their own.

The Hittites are apprehensive to make him an equal by selling him land and so continue their offer, but Abraham is not persuaded. He pushes the point and ends up buying the land from the man Ephron for a significant amount of money. The chapter closes with Abraham successfully burying his wife in the cave he now owns, and the author foreshadows this as the beginning of God's fulfillment of the promise of land.

Slowly but surely, the readers of Genesis are seeing the promises of God to Abraham fulfilled, but usually in timeframes and circumstances that are monumentally different than expected. In this chapter, Abraham acted out of love and honor and received the beginnings of a promise as a reward, but it's hard to believe that was his only intention. He loved his wife tremendously and acted in her best interest as well as in the interest of his family (because he and his children would end up being buried there as well.)

Sometimes following God's will looks exactly like normal life. Making choices without knowing which one is correct, dealing with personalities and circumstances to find a suitable outcome, and just trying and praying and letting things fall where they will.

The Christian life is, for the most part, not supernatural. What Christ and the Holy Spirit did and do is certainly beyond this world. But on our part, most of what we do will be classified as normal. Normal prayers, normal errands, normal difficulties and frustrations, and normal successes. It's God who takes the normal and turns it into supernatural. All Abraham did was honor his wife and buy a piece of land. God allowed those things to happen but then went further and used that one event to start the ripple effect that enabled Israel to become its own kingdom.

God takes our normal and *Christifies* it – exploding it into eternal significance, just as He did with the people we read about in the Bible. We just need to be faithful in the normal and rely on Him to do the rest.

Takeaway: God takes our faithful normal and makes it supernatural.

Prayer: Help me be faithful in the day-to-day of this life, Lord, so that You can make extraordinary things come from it.

Legacy of Trust

Day 26
Genesis 24:1-9

These verses capture the last spoken words of Abraham. After decades of pursuing the promises of God and watching as He miraculously provided, Abraham sets his sights on securing his legacy. Isaac is of marrying age and Abraham wants to ensure that his future descendants will be from the right bloodline and live in the right location so as to fulfill the promises of God.

Abraham calls upon his most trusted servant to go find his son a wife. This is no ordinary request. The servant knows that, even in the best circumstances, this will be difficult to accomplish, so he asks what will happen if he fails. Abraham is a little surprised by the servant's question and responds as the man of faith he has grown into: *God has kept all His promises so far, He will make a way for this to work as well.*

The servant accepts the matter, then the two men seal the request in a sacred way, by placing the servant's hand underneath Abraham's thigh to signify the importance of the task. If the servant

73

succeeded, he would initiate the next phase of God's promises and the birth of the tribes of Israel.

Just as Abraham's story began before he ever set foot upon this earth, so his story will continue on after his days are over. Isaac is now the man God will use to fulfill His promises and bring to fruition the blessing to all peoples.

Abraham did his part. He trusted God, even when it was difficult, even when he had just disobeyed him. Abraham always came back saying, *okay God let's do this Your way.*

I can't help but believe that Isaac saw at least a little of that in his father, enough to convince him that trusting God was always the best option. As time went on, Isaac kept and shared those stories, engraining it into his own children, and they passed it on to their children, and so on.

Abraham built his legacy by remaining faithful one day at a time. He didn't exult himself or preach about his accomplishments. Instead, he let people learn from his life what they saw to be true. You are building your legacy whether you know it or not. The way you treat other people, the way you trust God with money or work or family, the attitude you portray – you have an audience for everything you do, whether you realize it or not. Ultimately our legacy comes down to a single question: did we trust God?

For Abraham the answer was yes – and that started a series of events no one could have dreamed. What will your legacy be?

Takeaway: I am building my legacy every day in the way I trust God or not.

Prayer: Father, help me trust You even in the smallest things, so that my life will be characterized and driven by faith and not by fear.

Infectious Faith

Day 27
Genesis 24:10-61

The stage is set for Abraham's servant to fulfill his oath. He gathers what he needs and prays a very specific prayer. The servant wants the girl God has chosen to offer to water his camels once he arrives: an odd request, but exactly what is needed to make her stand out from the crowd.

The servant doesn't have to wait long once he arrives. Rebekah comes and fulfills the prayer with her offer to help. On top of that, she is even closer in bloodline than he could have hoped. Everything is working out great; now the servant just needs her family to cooperate.

Rebekah's brother dominates the next scene. He is the leading male in the household (the father is probably very old at this point), and his motivations are solely based on greed. He sees an opportunity to benefit from his sister's marriage and throughout the scene makes that point clear.

Next the reader experiences a very long, detailed retelling of everything that has happened up to this point. Why is this necessary? We are seeing the servant persuade his hearers. He wants to make his goal very clear but also hint that everyone there will be better off for making this deal. The extended speech works, and the marriage is blessed.

One final roadblock lies before the servant's success. The family beckons him to let Rebekah stay for a while, but he will not have this. He wants to hurry and fulfill his promise before anything else can get in the way. Thankfully, Rebekah agrees to leave that very day to fulfill the promise and meet Isaac.

This is one of the longest stories, and one can get lost within its details. But after spending weeks with Abraham, the aspect of legacy comes to mind once again. Abraham's legacy of faith impacted everyone around him.

The servant was at first overwhelmed at the request to find a bride for Isaac. But he made an oath and committed to it. He prayed to God for a clear sign, and when he saw it, he knew God had stepped in to help.

Rebekah was greeted by a wealthy stranger at the well, and the next day she left with him to meet her future husband. That took extreme faith: believing that God had her best in mind.

Because Abraham walked in faith, others had the courage to do so also. Abraham's faith encouraged the faith of his servant, whose faith in turn prompted Rebekah's. Your faith, or lack of it, will greatly impact those around you. Think about what kind of ripple effect your legacy will leave.

Takeaway: Our faith impacts the faith of others.

Prayer: Father help me to be a walking example of a man of faith, so that those I care about most will grow in their faith as well.

Imagining Greatness

Day 28
Genesis 24:62-67

Finally, all the elements for the line of Abraham to continue are in place. Isaac spots an approaching party just as Rebekah spots him in the field. The servant confirms that this is the man she has left everything behind to meet.

Once again the servant shares his story, this time with Isaac, to bring him up to date about everything that has occurred. As you could imagine, he is probably elated. His father acted for his best interest and now here was this beautiful young woman he could finally call his own.

The two are married. So as Isaac's story begins, Abraham's comes to a close.

You can't help but read this passage and feel a mounting sense of relief. They did it! God did it! He kept all of His promises despite everything in the world saying it couldn't happen - despite delay and hardship, doubt and conflict, hopelessness and failure. This scene is what God had in mind from the very first day He spoke to Abraham. This is what

God wanted His servant to imagine, to keep him going and hoping when things got tough.

Some people believe Abraham did not live to see this moment, that he passed away before the servant returned from his journey.[iv] However, I believe Abraham did live to see it. I believe Abraham celebrated the marriage with his son and new daughter-in-law. That he praised God that night and laughed at all the challenges they overcame to reach that point.

God saw His promises come true, He knew what was to come. Imagining their reality can help us have faith like Abraham, like his servant, and like Isaac. Impossible futures for us are only matter of time to God. Our hopes are His plans.

Takeaway: Imagining God's provision strengthens our faith.

Prayer: Thank You Lord, that You have an incredible future for me. Build in my mind the image of hope You want me to foster.

Lord, Lead Me

Day 29
Genesis 25:1-11

The final scene of Abraham's life is likely not chronological.[v] He likely married Keturah long before Sarah passed, just as he had Hagar earlier in life. By moving this little fact to the end the writer was able to keep attention on the main storyline, and then at the end show additional ways in which God fulfilled His promises.

Abraham had many more children who each became their own tribes and peoples. However, Isaac was still the main son - the one who inherited everything and became the nation God would eventually use to change the course of history.

After wrapping up the final details, our patriarch passes in peace. He is laid to rest by both Isaac and Ishmael in the tomb with his wife Sarah. And so the story of this great man comes to rest, once he is old and accomplished and has lived to see the hand of God prevail.

Abraham will be remembered as a man of God despite the poor decisions he made at times. Above all he was human, but his humanity did not define him. Instead, he was able to accomplish so much and carry extraordinary influence because he trusted God in a way that is almost foreign to us – with complete abandon. No safety nets, no backup plans. Abraham went all in: traveling to foreign countries, battling kings, standing back up after he had fallen and growing into one of the wealthiest men at that time.

Abraham let God define him. God took his desire to be a father and elevated it to a father of nations. Abraham trusted God to guide his life and then walked in such a way that God had to show up for these things to come true.

We all want to die like Abraham: old, fulfilled and rich. But how many of us are willing to live like him? To trust God without abandon, to let Him define what we will be and what we should pursue?

The God who led Abraham is the same God we serve today, and He is waiting for people to rise up and say "I am yours, lead me."

Takeaway: Abraham's life was a product of God's providence.

Prayer: Lord, keep me from a life where I am completely in control. Define me, lead me, and make me great for Your purposes.

Stories of Faith

Day 30
Romans 4:16

"Therefore, the promise comes by faith, so that it may be by grace and may be guaranteed to all Abraham's offspring – not only to those who are of the law but also to those who have the faith of Abraham. He is the father of us all."

Our stories are stories of faith.

We place faith in jobs, education, people, and in ourselves with the hope that these forces will fulfill our hearts and provide us with the lives we desperately want. Yet we often find ourselves stuck and frustrated, exhausted by our own pursuits and dissatisfied with the results.

Abraham succeeded because he put his faith in the right thing. He trusted God to be his source and fulfillment, and allowed God to write the script for his life instead of trying to fashion one on his own.

This is how we succeed and are saved: by placing our faith in the right One, and believing in His guidance.

Becoming the person our family and friends need starts with allowing God to become who we need.

I hope the example of Abraham's life and faith will encourage you. He was a man just like me, just like you. God is waiting to start your adventure. I hope you'll take the challenge.

Takeaway: We are always putting our faith in something.

Prayer: Thank You Lord, that You have an extraordinary plan for my life. Pease give me the faith to pursue it.

Continuing the Journey

Thank you for reading Climbing with Abraham. I hope the experience was encouraging and that you've learned just a little bit more about one of the greatest characters in the Old Testament.

Now that you've started to dive into some Old Testament truths, here are two steps you can take to continue your journey.

First, sign up for my newsletter at RamosAuthor.com. Here you'll receive a monthly exclusive email. This is where I will be giving away free copies of new releases as they come out, along with other valuable insights.

Second, please write a short review for *Climbing with Abraham*. These reviews help me craft better, more effective books so I would deeply appreciate your support!

Of all the lessons I learned from Abraham, the one I keep coming back to is that our stories continue beyond us. Abraham was just the beginning. God continued to use his son Isaac, and then his son Jacob, to accomplish his promises. Fast-forward thousands of years and here we are – the long descended children of Abraham by faith and God is still working out His promises through us.

I hope you'll accept the call to become a part of God's never-ending story.

About the Author

David Ramos is an author and teacher passionate about communicating the life-changing truths found in the Old Testament. He has a degree in Classical and Medieval Studies and is currently finishing a Master's in Religion (Biblical Studies) at Ashland Theological Seminary. When he's not writing you can usually find David chasing down the newest food truck or helping his fiancé Breahna plan their wedding.

David and his library currently reside in Cleveland, Ohio.

Visit his website at RamosAuthor.com or follow him on Twitter @RamosAuthor.

More Books by David Ramos

Escaping with Jacob: 30 Devotionals to Help You Find Your Identity, Forgive Your Past, and Walk in Your Purpose

Enduring with Job: 30 Devotionals to Give You Hope, Stir Your Faith, and Find God's Power in Your Pain

The God with a Plan

Twentyfive: Treasures from an Unusual Millennial Life

The Shadow of Gethsemane: An Easter Poem

FURTHER READING ON ABRAHAM

Abraham by Bruce Feiler

An Introduction to the Old Testament by Walter Brueggemann
*Abraham is covered on pages 43-51

Genesis 1-15 (Volume 1) and *Genesis 16-50* (Volume 2) of *Word Biblical Commentary* by Gordon Wenham

The Book of Genesis (Chapters 18-50) of *The New International Commentary on the Old Testament* by Victor P/ Hamilton

Takeaway List

1. My story is part of a much bigger story.
2. My perspective of every situation will either encourage or dishearten my trust in God.
3. God knows I will make mistakes, but His promises are invincible.
4. As a child of God I am responsible for more than just myself.
5. It's okay to get frustrated when God doesn't seem to be keeping His promises. He's working on something big and has not forgotten about you.
6. Sometimes choosing God's best requires us to give up our immediate good.
7. God blesses us when we help fellow believers.
8. God knows your frustration; keep believing.
9. It's okay to ask God, *How can I know?* Faith doesn't always have to be invisible.

10. God's plans are not always logical, but they are the best option.

11. God sees me, and what He sees He takes action on.

12. Only God can fulfill the promises He makes.

13. God will ask difficult things of us at times; trust Him anyways.

14. Our relationship with God affects everyone around us.

15. Nothing is too difficult for God.

16. God is inviting us to change this world.

17. Prayer works, just not always in the way we think it should.

18. Remembering God's actions in our past will help us fight today's fear.

19. Put your faith in the Promisor, and keep your eyes on Him.

20. God doesn't run away from messes. He runs towards them.

21. God's promises require both patience and action.

22. God is our ultimate provider. God's actions are always for our provision.
23. My obedience, while difficult, is an incredibly powerful tool for God.
24. Marriage can be a tool for helping us fulfill the promises of God.
25. God takes our faithful normal and makes it supernatural.
26. I am building my legacy every day in the way I trust God or not.
27. Our faith impacts the faith of others.
28. Imagining God's provision strengthens our faith.
29. Abraham's life was a product of God's providence.
30. We are always putting our faith in something.

Acknowledgements

I would like to express my thanks to everyone who enabled this book to become a reality.

To my fiancé Breahna, for her incredible support and for never letting me give up. Also, I want to thank my mother and brother for sending their encouragement and prayers every time I needed them.

This book would have never come together without the help of two very important people: Bekah and Vikiana. They are experts of their crafts and I am deeply grateful for their help.

Thank you to every professor and pastor who challenged me to ask hard questions, and who enabled me to handle the Word of God with respect and skill.

Finally, I thank God for the opportunity to share His message with others. Everything I am is because of who He is.

Endnotes

[i] Gordon Wenham, *Genesis 16-50*, vol. 2 of *Word Biblical Commentary* (Dallas: Word Books, 1994), 9.

[ii] Ibid., 47.

[iii] Ibid., 129.

[iv] Ibid., 151.

[v] Ibid., 160.

Made in the USA
Middletown, DE
16 June 2016